# BR
# WA
## & Au

C000000290

**HMS Kent**

# THE ROYAL NAVY

**Each year we invite a well respected and informed defence journalist to introduce this book as a "guest author" - outlining how they see the current naval scene. This year we welcome Richard Scott, an internationally respected naval journalist.**

*"We are in a rapidly changing world and, for the Royal Navy, there is undoubtedly much further change to come. Society has changed, warfare has changed, the task has changed and the Navy of the 21st Century must undoubtedly change too. This will mean balancing some traditional behaviour against the needs of the times - and some of the former may not survive. Where this happens we must accept it gracefully, while maintaining throughout the essential elements of the ethos of the Navy. This represents a strong tradition which can sustain fighting spirit based around professionalism, courage, achievement and flexibility."*

The introduction to the Royal Navy's Strategic Plan 2000-2015, from which the excerpt above is taken, does not disguise the power of the social, political, fiscal and technological dynamics acting upon the service in the modern era. And yet at the same time it reveals the stark dichotomy facing the Navy Board as it attempts to identify what are, and what are not, those crucial ingredients necessary to maintain the RN as an effective fighting force into the 21st century.

As the Strategic Plan itself notes, three quite different but equally important forces are at work. The first is financial. Defence funding has been on a continuous downward spiral since the end of the Cold War, and the slight increase announced in the Comprehensive Defence Review in October 2000 does not signal any fundamental change. Education, health and transport will remain the priorities of this or any other government for the foreseeable future.

According to the Strategic Plan, this means "continued pressure to demonstrate ever greater value for money and efficiency." Economies, savings measures or cutbacks by any other name.

The next factor is employment. "There will be a declining number of people in the age groups from which we traditionally recruit and hence increasing difficulty in recruiting sufficient numbers of the right quality people into the Navy and retaining them. There will be an increasing need for more technically competent servicemen and women at all levels. Employment patterns generally indicate a trend towards individuals seeking more flexible, more self-managed careers."

To this end, the RN in November 2000 launched its "policy for people", an initiative intended to improve quality of life for service personnel and their families. Its aims, championed by the Second Sea Lord, are laudable, but how they are reconciled with the demands being placed upon the service's men and women will be worth watching. Short-notice contingency deployments have become more frequent, and the navy's personnel underbearing means many billets are still left "gapped", increasing workload and damaging morale.

The third key dynamic is technology. "The rapid pace of technological change will make demands on the way in which the Navy conducts its business, its management structures, the conduct of operations and the upgrading of fighting capability. The Navy will need to be able to adapt, quickly, to this changing environment."

In practice, this could mean quite radical changes to the planning, conduct and sustainment of operations. The Strategic Plan suggests as follows: "The tempo of operations is likely to intensify with digitisation of the battlespace, and with the introduction of "sensor to shooter" capabilities reducing the decision cycle. Operating patterns of warships themselves may be substantially different. Improving maintenance philosophies and methods will result in higher availability being achieved from ships. New ships and new aircraft could therefore spend longer on task, requiring a balance between this greater operational flexibility and a radically different approach to manning and thus new methods of managing harmony."

"Increased use of synthetic training facilities will be needed both ashore and afloat to assure operational effectiveness. The joint nature of future operations places increasing importance on a number of joint enabling capabilities, particularly electronic warfare, command and control, intelligence, surveillance, target acquisition and reconnaissance, strategic lift and combat service support."

It is in these very areas where so many shortfalls currently exist. But with equipment budgets being squeezed, how will these much sought-after new capabilities be brought into service, and in what timescale? It is here where the long-range vision becomes increasingly blurred.

No one can argue that the Strategic Plan has failed to identify the key dynamics. The problem, as ever, is in attempting to square these long-term issues with the short-term foreign and security policy objectives of the incumbent government. Long on rhetoric and short on memory, politicians of both major parties have continually paid lip service to the stability in resourcing which the armed forces so desperately need as they re-shape to meet post-Cold War requirements.

For the RN, this wholesale change in doctrinal development and operational planning is enshrined in the operational concept of the Maritime Contribution to Joint Operations (MCJO), first laid out in the 1998 Strategic Defence Review (SDR). As the Strategic Plan summarises: "There will continue to be evolutionary changes to warfare itself, with increased emphasis on information management, precision engagement, rapid deployability, poise and responses to asymmetric threats. Major operations are likely to be undertaken in concert with allies, particularly US and NATO forces, and greater pan-European involvement in many operations can be anticipated in the period. The emphasis for the Navy will be on expeditionary and littoral warfare, and our contribution to joint and combined operations, particularly at small and medium scales of effort."

Mention of pan-European operations foreshadowed the November 2000 announcement that the UK would earmark a substantial force - including 18 warships - to a new European Union (EU) Rapid Reaction Force. Europe's inability to act quickly and decisively in Kosovo without US support has driven the move, and in that regard it is to be welcomed. But the initiative has generated distinct uneasiness in some quarters, on the grounds that it may undermine or usurp NATO in the longer term. Also, there is no sign that any EU nations - including the UK - are prepared to commit any additional funding to redress critical force overstetch and capability shortfalls.

Therein lies a persistent theme. SDR, MCJO and similar have articulated worthy policy and doctrinal frameworks. But the current high operational tempo is putting existing material and naval personnel under exceptional strain, and at the same time eroding the equipment budget. The corollary is that the new force architectures and equipment capabilities fundamental to SDR simply cannot be delivered in anything close to the timescales envisioned.

Equipment problems were very much to the fore as the fleet went about its business in the first year of this new millennium. Poor availability continues to dog elements of maritime aviation, and the submarine service experienced something of an *"annus horriblis"* on the eve of its centenary after a series of breakdowns and safety scares. This was all the more galling after the success of HMS SPLENDID and Tomahawk in the Kosovo campaign the previous year.

Nevertheless, the RN was able to demonstrate - at a stretch - the broad spectrum of capabilities it can still deploy at a global scale in support of UK interests. Mid-January 2000 saw a task group led by HMS ILLUSTRIOUS set sail for the Gulf for training and exercises in the region. In March the auxiliary oiler replenishment vessel RFA FORT GEORGE, with five Sea Kings embarked, was detached from the group to deploy off Mozambique in support of flood relief efforts, illustrating the versatility of systems and capabilities designed for war but finding more frequent utility in peace and crisis.

Naval Task Group (NTG) 2000, comprising the frigates HMS CORNWALL and HMS SUTHERLAND, the destroyer HMS NEWCASTLE and the auxiliaries RFA FORT VICTORIA and RFA BAYLEAF, left UK waters in the spring to participate in a series of exercises in the Mediterranean, the Middle East and the Asia Pacific region. Returning via the Panama Canal, the circumnavigating group signalled the UK's continued commitment towards the Five Power Defence Arrangement and wider regional stability. Integrated within the force for the seven-month deployment was the French frigate ACONIT, a very visible demonstration of the increasingly close bonds being forged between the RN and the Marine National in recent years.

HMS TIRELESS sailed with NTG 2000, but the discovery in May of a coolant leak in its reactor primary circuit while in the Mediterranean saw the submarine withdrawn from the deployment and brought alongside in Gibraltar. The ramifications of this defect, both political and operational, were only to become apparent in the following months.

Mine countermeasures vessels, so often left in the shadows, were also deployed far and wide into the Gulf, the Mediterranean, the Black Sea and the Baltic. Their contribution to power projection operations should not be underplayed, particularly their vital role in support of amphibious forces. Mention should also be made of HMS SCOTT, now well into a survey deployment to the Atlantic and the Indian Ocean which will last almost two years.

During the summer the carrier HMS INVINCIBLE was the centrepiece of the round-UK "Meet Your Navy" deployment, a six-week programme of port visits involving 26 warships of all types. It offered a chance for over 57,000 people to go aboard HM ships, raising public awareness regarding the role of the modern RN, and also providing an excellent vehicle for the recruiters.

INVINCIBLE was subsequently deployed to the Adriatic to demonstrate the UK's "resolve" should Serbia (then still in the clutches of the Milosevic regime) attempt to interfere in the elections in neighbouring Montenegro. The carrier's helicopters were later to play a major role in the search and rescue operation following the sinking of a Greek ferry off the island of Paros.

But without doubt the most significant deployment undertaken during the past year was Operation "Palliser", the UK's intervention in the West African state of Sierra Leone. "Palliser" represented a coming of age for the concept of the Joint Rapid Reaction Forces (under the command of the Permanent Joint Headquarters) and saw the first major operational test for the UK's new joint-service approach to maritime aviation. It was also a purely national operation, something which defence planners should bear in mind when making assumptions on future force requirements.

The maritime contribution was led by HMS ILLUSTRIOUS, embarking a mixed bag of 13 Harrier GR.7s and Sea Harrier FA.2s from the newly-formed Joint Force Harrier, and the helicopter carrier (LPH) HMS OCEAN, centrepiece of an eight-ship Amphibious Ready Group (ARG), with 42 Commando Royal Marines and a mix of Sea King HC.4, Lynx and Gazelle helicopters. Other units included HMS CHATHAM, HMS ARGYLL, RFA FORT GEORGE, RFA SIR PERCIVALE, RFA SIR TRISTRAM and RFA SIR BEDIVERE.

In November 2000 the ARG was once again deployed off the coast of Sierra Leone. While many continue to voice doubts over the rationale for the UK's deepening involvement in Sierra Leone's civil war, events off West Africa have reminded politicians of all persuasions of the unique attributes which amphibious forces afford the joint force commander in peacetime, crisis and conflict. Logistically self-sufficient and politically benign, they require no rights of passage, yet their mere departure from port may in itself send an important message. Furthermore, the force can remain poised over the horizon for a prolonged period, and can be quickly withdrawn, re-deployed or committed to meet the needs of an evolving crisis situation.

HMS OCEAN in particular has shown herself to be a most versatile asset. Her first couple of years in service have not been without problems, due in part to the ship's hybrid mix of military and commercial standards, but the value of having a dedicated LPH is quite evident. Indeed, there is a strong case to be made for a second purpose-built LPH, learning from the lessons of OCEAN, and ending once and for all the far from satisfactory expedient of substituting an Invincible class carrier into the LPH role when OCEAN is unavailable.

Whether the ability to deploy a landing platform dock (LPD) in the front-line can be maintained up until the late-running LPD replacement vessels ALBION and BULWARK enter service is in serious doubt. FEARLESS has soldiered on gamely, but her material condition is poor and support and manning requirements extremely costly. An engine room fire sustained after exercises in the Mediterranean during November left the ship making temporary repairs at Malta, and once again prompted speculation as to whether she might be paid off early.

Also stranded in the Mediterranean for much of the year was HMS TIRELESS. The decision to repair the boat in Gibraltar caused much consternation amid the local population and the Spanish government. But worse was to come when repair work revealed that the defect could be generic to all Swiftsure and Trafalgar class submarines. This prompted the recall of the entire SSN fleet in October, a move which sparked a wave of negative publicity for the submarine service. Sadly, it also overshadowed the earlier efforts, albeit in vain, of the RN's submarine rescue service to rescue the crew of the stricken Russian submarine KURSK.

On the equipment front, there have been some welcome, if overdue, announcements. The go-ahead for the Type 45 air defence destroyer programme came in July, and an order for the first three (of a projected twelve) ships was expected by the end of 2000. Deploying the new Principal Anti-Air Missile System (PAAMS), this long awaited new class will replace the increasingly tired Type 42 destroyers. The first of class, HMS DARING, is due in service in late 2007.

Rapid progress on the Type 45 since the collapse of the collaborative Horizon frigate programme has shown that the much-vaunted Smart Procurement Initiative is producing some encouraging early success. Yet the good news must be tempered by the acknowledgement that cost constraints will see early Type 45s entering service devoid of many desirable equipments and capabilities. There is no place for a close-in weapon system, anti-ship missiles or magazine-launched torpedoes, and doubts remain whether the budget for the first batch will stretch to a medium-frequency bow sonar.

After much political procrastination, a consortium led by Andrew Weir Shipping was selected to provide the MoD's strategic sealift service under a Private Finance Initiative (PFI) arrangement lasting almost 25 years. The fact that only two of the six Ro-Ro vessels will be built in a UK yard has understandably aggrieved regional lobbies and unions alike. It is unlikely that any other European government would have insisted on so scrupulously observing EU and World Trade Organisation rules.

The fact that a planned order for two new Alternative Landing Ship Logistic (ALSL) vessels was doubled to four had more to do with regional politics than enlightened defence planning, but was a nonetheless welcome development. Indeed, the ALSL programme stands out as an example of "smart" procurement, the chosen design displaying many characteristics more typical of an LPD.

Two new multi-role hydrographic and oceanographic survey vessels were at long last ordered, to enter service in 2002 and 2003. As well as providing both hydrographic and oceanographic survey data, they will also offer combat survey and mine warfare support capabilities.

According to the MoD, both ships will be available for operations for more than 330 days each year, a 50% improvement on older existing vessels. They will also offer much improved seakeeping, enabling them to spend a far higher percentage of time at sea in rough conditions than current ships.

Mention should also be made of the trimaran demonstrator RV TRITON which began its trials programme with the Defence Evaluation and Research Agency (DERA) in October 2000. Over the next 18 months, the vessel will conduct a programme of sea trials intended to characterise the structural and hydrodynamic performance of the catamaran hullform in a large-scale warship application.

Should the results of sea trials bear out the claimed advantages of the trimaran over an equivalent monohull (lower powering requirements, improved seakeeping, an increase in upper deck area providing more space for aviation facilities and weapons, and a wider helicopter operating envelope), then this novel hullform could be selected for the RN's next-generation Future Surface Combatant . Meanwhile, TRITON will find gainful employment in the longer term as a general purpose trials platform for DERA.

Rival industry teams led by BAE Systems and Thomson-CSF have been continuing the assessment study phase activities for the Future Aircraft Carrier (CVF) programme. By the end of 2000 it appeared that the Joint Strike Fighter had emerged as the preferred "strike fighter" for the new carriers, but judgement was being reserved on whether to opt for short-take off/vertical landing or catapult launch/arrested recovery. This decision will condition the final design selected for the two CVF ships, each likely to displace something in excess of 40,000 tons.

Work has started on the fabrication of HMS ASTUTE, the first of a new class of SSN to enter service from 2005. Three boats are on order, and it is hoped that an order for a second batch of three will follow in late 2002. Originally a class of five Astute class SSNs was planned: the sixth boat has been brought into the programme as a coherency measure to realise significant whole life cost savings (achieved at the expense of a further Trafalgar class refuelling).

Perhaps the single most significant new equipment acquisition announced during the course of 2000 went largely unsung. In June the US government agreed to share a revolutionary new radar networking technology with the UK in a move which promises to dramatically increase the effectiveness and survivability of the RN's surface fleet. It marks the first time that the US government

6

has been prepared to release this highly sensitive technology overseas.

The system, known as the Cooperative Engagement Capability (CEC) allows suitably-equipped surface ships and aircraft to exchange real-time radar data on air targets, allowing them to function as an integrated air defence network. It improves detection, tracking and identification of air targets, increases defensive coverage, and enables comprehensive force-wide coordination among a group of warships.

For the RN, access to CEC is extremely important. The increasing speed and stealth of aircraft and anti-ship missiles demands improved "situational awareness" for UK maritime forces engaged in independent or coalition operations. UK participation in CEC will also maintain high-level interoperability between RN and US Navy warships, something which will be essential in future coalition operations.

CEC should enter service with the RN in about 2008. Type 23 frigates will be the first RN ships equipped with CEC, with the new Type 45 destroyers to follow in due course.

As the year drew to a close, there were signs that moves were afoot to proceed with a five-to-ten year PFI deal to provide new ships and support to the RN's Fishery Protection Squadron. The so-called Future Offshore Patrol Vessel (FOPV) programme is intended to replace the capability currently provided by the RN's five Island class OPVs.

To conclude, one goes back to the RN Strategic Plan and its accompanying mission statement, "A world class navy, ready to fight and win." It is a bold message, and one with which all the service can readily identify. Whether it is tuned into the right political wavelength is an altogether different matter.

While ministers have become increasingly quick to deploy forces in support of foreign policy objectives, it appears that they can quickly become uncomfortable with the warfighting options presented to them. Aircraft carriers are the prime case in point: the presence of HMS ILLUSTRIOUS off Sierra Leone was played down right up until the ship's return to the UK less her presence off West Africa was interpreted as "inappropriate" force. It should ring alarm bells to those in higher command as they prepare to deploy arguments in justification of the CVF programme.

At least the man at the top will be prepared to argue the maritime case. The appointment of Admiral Sir Michael Boyce as Chief of the Defence Staff offers the navy a most welcome, if long overdue, opportunity to reaffirm the case for the new carriers as the centrepiece of future joint expeditionary operations.

It is important that he and his colleagues should be able to have the public at large on their side, and it is here where the initiative of Vice Admiral Sir Roy Newman, president of the Royal Naval Association, is to be applauded. In an interview with *Navy News* published last October he called for the multitude of ex-service organisations, nautical charities, maritime volunteer groups and other associations to consider coming together under the umbrella of a strong Navy League, akin to those long established in the USA and Australia.

There exists a host of issues to be resolved, but it is a timely and appropriate initiative. The RN must be better understood by the taxpayer who funds it, and hence better placed to draw on the support of the media and population at large. A strong and energetic Navy League would provide a clear voice for all those who understand the vital importance of the RN's contribution to the UK's defence policy into the 21st century. It is a goal well worth pursuing.


Richard Scott

December 2000

# SHIPS OF THE ROYAL NAVY
## Pennant Numbers

| Ship | Pennant Number | Page | Ship | Pennant Number | Page |
|---|---|---|---|---|---|
| **Aircraft Carriers** | | | | | |
| | | | CORNWALL | F99 | 20 |
| INVINCIBLE | R05 | 14 | LANCASTER | F229 | 21 |
| ILLUSTRIOUS | R06 | 14 | NORFOLK | F230 | 21 |
| ARK ROYAL | R07 | 14 | ARGYLL | F231 | 21 |
| | | | MARLBOROUGH | F233 | 21 |
| **Destroyers** | | | IRON DUKE | F234 | 21 |
| | | | MONMOUTH | F235 | 21 |
| NEWCASTLE | D87 | 17 | MONTROSE | F236 | 21 |
| GLASGOW | D88 | 17 | WESTMINSTER | F237 | 21 |
| EXETER | D89 | 17 | NORTHUMBERLAND | F238 | 21 |
| SOUTHAMPTON | D90 | 17 | RICHMOND | F239 | 21 |
| NOTTINGHAM | D91 | 17 | | | |
| LIVERPOOL | D92 | 17 | **Submarines** | | |
| MANCHESTER | D95 | 18 | | | |
| GLOUCESTER | D96 | 18 | VANGUARD | S28 | 10 |
| EDINBURGH | D97 | 18 | VICTORIOUS | S29 | 10 |
| YORK | D98 | 18 | VIGILANT | S30 | 10 |
| CARDIFF | D108 | 17 | VENGEANCE | S31 | 10 |
| | | | UPHOLDER ● | S40 | 13 |
| **Frigates** | | | URSULA ● | S42 | 13 |
| | | | UNICORN ● | S43 | 13 |
| KENT | F78 | 21 | TRENCHANT | S91 | 11 |
| PORTLAND | F79 | 21 | TALENT | S92 | 11 |
| GRAFTON | F80 | 21 | TRIUMPH | S93 | 11 |
| SUTHERLAND | F81 | 21 | SCEPTRE | S104 | 12 |
| SOMERSET | F82 | 21 | SPARTAN | S105 | 12 |
| ST ALBANS | F83 | 21 | SPLENDID | S106 | 12 |
| CUMBERLAND | F85 | 20 | TRAFALGAR | S107 | 11 |
| CAMPBELTOWN | F86 | 20 | SOVEREIGN | S108 | 12 |
| CHATHAM | F87 | 20 | SUPERB | S109 | 12 |
| BRAVE | F94 | 19 | TURBULENT | S110 | 11 |
| SHEFFIELD | F96 | 19 | TIRELESS | S117 | 11 |
| COVENTRY | F98 | 19 | TORBAY | S118 | 11 |

| Ship | Pennant Number | Page | Ship | Pennant Number | Page |
|---|---|---|---|---|---|
| **Assault Ships** | | | | | |
| FEARLESS | L10 | 16 | SMITER | P272 | 27 |
| OCEAN | L12 | 15 | PURSUER | P273 | 27 |
| | | | TRACKER | P274 | 27 |
| **Minehunters** | | | RAIDER | P275 | 27 |
| | | | ANGLESEY | P277 | 26 |
| BRECON | M29 | 23 | ALDERNEY | P278 | 26 |
| LEDBURY | M30 | 23 | BLAZER | P279 | 27 |
| CATTISTOCK | M31 | 23 | DASHER | P280 | 27 |
| COTTESMORE | M32 | 23 | PUNCHER | P291 | 27 |
| BROCKLESBY | M33 | 23 | CHARGER | P292 | 27 |
| MIDDLETON | M34 | 23 | RANGER | P293 | 27 |
| DULVERTON | M35 | 23 | TRUMPETER | P294 | 27 |
| CHIDDINGFOLD | M37 | 23 | GUERNSEY | P297 | 26 |
| ATHERSTONE | M38 | 23 | SHETLAND | P298 | 26 |
| HURWORTH | M39 | 23 | LINDISFARNE | P300 | 26 |
| BERKELEY | M40 | 23 | | | |
| QUORN | M41 | 23 | **Survey Ships & RN Manned Auxiliaries** | | |
| SANDOWN | M101 | 24 | | | |
| INVERNESS | M102 | 24 | GLEANER | H86 | 32 |
| CROMER | M103 | 24 | ROEBUCK | H130 | 29 |
| WALNEY | M104 | 24 | SCOTT | H131 | 28 |
| BRIDPORT | M105 | 24 | HERALD | H138 | 30 |
| PENZANCE | M106 | 24 | EXPRESS | A163 | 34 |
| PEMBROKE | M107 | 24 | EXPLORER | A164 | 34 |
| GRIMSBY | M108 | 24 | EXAMPLE | A165 | 34 |
| BANGOR | M109 | 24 | EXPLOIT | A167 | 34 |
| | | | ENDURANCE | A171 | 33 |
| **Patrol Craft** | | | IRONBRIDGE | A311 | 73 |
| | | | BULLDOG | H317 | 31 |
| LEEDS CASTLE | P258 | 25 | IXWORTH | A318 | 73 |
| ARCHER | P264 | 27 | BEAGLE | H319 | 31 |
| DUMBARTON CASTLE | P265 | 25 | | | |
| BITER | P270 | 27 | ● *Ships in reserve/long refit* | | |

● DAVE CULLEN

**HMS Vigilant**

# VANGUARD CLASS

| Ship | Pennant Number | Completion Date | Builder |
|------|----------------|-----------------|---------|
| VANGUARD | S28 | 1992 | VSEL |
| VICTORIOUS | S29 | 1994 | VSEL |
| VIGILANT | S30 | 1997 | VSEL |
| VENGEANCE | S31 | 1999 | VSEL |

**Displacement** 15,000 tons (dived) **Dimensions** 150m x 13m x 12m **Speed** 25 + dived
**Armament** 16 - Trident 2 (D5) missiles, 4 Torpedo Tubes **Complement** 135

**Notes**
After the first UK successful D5 strategic missile firing in May '94 the first operational
patrol was carried out in early '95 and a patrol has been constantly maintained ever since.
These submarines have two crews each to maintain the maximum period on patrol.
Construction costs of the last, VENGEANCE, are estimated at £863 million.

10

HMS Triumph

# TRAFALGAR CLASS

| Ship | Pennant Number | Completion Date | Builder |
|------|----------------|-----------------|---------|
| TRENCHANT | S91 | 1989 | Vickers |
| TALENT | S92 | 1990 | Vickers |
| TRIUMPH | S93 | 1991 | Vickers |
| TRAFALGAR | S107 | 1983 | Vickers |
| TURBULENT | S110 | 1984 | Vickers |
| TIRELESS | S117 | 1985 | Vickers |
| TORBAY | S118 | 1986 | Vickers |

**Displacement** 4,500 tons **Dimensions** 85m x 10m x 8m **Speed** 30 + dived **Armament** 5 Torpedo Tubes **Complement** 125.

### Notes
Enhanced development of the Swiftsure Class. Quieter, faster and with greater endurance than their predecessors. It is expected Tomahawk Cruise Missiles will eventually be fitted in all of these boats. Three new Batch II Trafalgar Class vessels (to be named ASTUTE, ARTFUL and AMBUSH) were ordered in March 1997.

11

**HMS Superb**

## SWIFTSURE CLASS

| Ship | Pennant Number | Completion Date | Builder |
|------|----------------|-----------------|---------|
| SCEPTRE | S104 | 1978 | Vickers |
| SPARTAN | S105 | 1979 | Vickers |
| SPLENDID | S106 | 1980 | Vickers |
| SOVEREIGN | S108 | 1974 | Vickers |
| SUPERB | S109 | 1976 | Vickers |

**Displacement** 4,500 tons dived **Dimensions** 83m x 10m x 8m **Speed** 30 knots + dived **Armament** 5 Torpedo Tubes **Complement** 116.

**Notes**
All are based at Faslane. The class will be replaced in due course by the Batch 2 Trafalgar class boats. It is anticipated that two vessels will be withdrawn from service in 2001/2 as a result of the Strategic Defence Review.

**HMS Unicorn**

# UPHOLDER CLASS

| Ship | Pennant Number | Completion Date | Builder |
|------|---------------|-----------------|---------|
| UPHOLDER | S40 | 1989 | Vickers |
| URSULA | S42 | 1992 | Cammell Laird |
| UNICORN | S43 | 1993 | Cammell Laird |

**Displacement** 2,400 tons (dived) **Dimensions** 70m x 8m x 5m **Speed** 20 knots dived **Armament** 6 Torpedo Tubes: Sub Harpoon missile **Complement** 44.

### Notes

A class of conventionally powered submarines. As a result of Defence economies announced in 1993 all the class were paid off during 1994 and laid up at Barrow-in-Furness in late 1998. They have been leased to Canada who started to take delivery in mid 2000. The first, UNSEEN, was renamed HMCS VICTORIA and arrived in Halifax, Nova Scotia in October 2000. Remainder to transfer by mid-2002.

● MIKE WELSFORD

**HMS Illustrious**

# INVINCIBLE CLASS

| Ship | Pennant Number | Completion Date | Builder |
|------|---------------|-----------------|---------|
| INVINCIBLE | R05 | 1979 | Vickers |
| ILLUSTRIOUS | R06 | 1982 | Swan Hunter |
| ARK ROYAL | R07 | 1985 | Swan Hunter |

**Displacement** 19,500 tons **Dimensions** 206m x 32m x 6.5m **Speed** 28 knots
**Armament** 2 - 20mm guns, 3 Phalanx/Goalkeeper **Aircraft** 8 - Sea Harrier, 12 - Sea
King (Merlin on ARK ROYAL) **Complement** 900 + aircrews.

**Notes**
Manpower problems have dictated that only two ships are kept in the operational fleet,
with the third in refit or reserve. ARK ROYAL entered long refit at Rosyth in mid 1999 and
is due to complete in Nov 2001. The original Sea Dart system has been removed from
all three carriers to increase deck space for more aircraft. It is uncertain how long
INVINCIBLE will be in operational service in 2001.

14

**HMS Ocean**

## LPH

| Ship | Pennant Number | Completion Date | Builder |
|------|----------------|-----------------|---------|
| OCEAN | L12 | 1998 | Kvaerner |

**Displacement** 21,578 tonnes **Dimensions** 208m x 34m x 6.6m **Speed** 19 knots **Armament** 3 x Phalanx, 6 x 30mm BMARC guns **Complement** Ship 298, Squadrons 180, Embarked force 800.

### Notes
The new Landing Platform (Helicopter) was launched in October 1995 at Kvaerner's yard in Glasgow and became fully operational in May 1999. Can carry 12 Sea King and 6 Lynx or Gazelle helicopters. Frequently employed as the flagship of the UK Amphibious Ready Group.

● MIKE WELSFORD

**HMS Fearless**

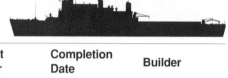

## FEARLESS CLASS

| Ship | Pennant Number | Completion Date | Builder |
| --- | --- | --- | --- |
| FEARLESS | L10 | 1965 | Harland & Wolff |
| INTREPID | L11 | 1967 | J. Brown |

**Displacement** 12,500 tons, 19,500 tons (flooded) **Dimensions** 158m x 24m x 8m
**Speed** 20 knots **Armament** 2 - Vulcan Phalanx (FEARLESS only) 2 - 20mm guns, 4 -
30mm **Complement** 580.

### Notes
Multi-purpose ships that can operate helicopters for embarked Royal Marine
Commandos. 4 landing craft are carried on an internal deck and are flooded out when
the ship docks down. INTREPID paid off at Portsmouth in 1991 and by 1996 £32 million
had been spent on maintenance since she paid off. That figure continued to rise until
1999 when she was placed in "extended readiness" with a much reduced ship's company. Financial restraints delayed any replacement order being made until 1996 when it was
announced that two new vessels were to be ordered and named ALBION and BULWARK.
(The first steel was cut in November 1997). Despite her age FEARLESS is expected to
be kept operational until Dec 2003 when the second vessel is due to be delivered.

16

**HMS Exeter**

# SHEFFIELD CLASS
## (Type 42) Batch 1 & 2

| Ship | Pennant Number | Completion Date | Builder |
|------|---------------|-----------------|---------|
| NEWCASTLE | D87 | 1978 | Swan Hunter |
| GLASGOW | D88 | 1978 | Swan Hunter |
| EXETER | D89 | 1980 | Swan Hunter |
| SOUTHAMPTON | D90 | 1981 | Vosper T. |
| NOTTINGHAM | D91 | 1982 | Vosper T. |
| LIVERPOOL | D92 | 1982 | C. Laird |
| CARDIFF | D108 | 1979 | Vickers |

**Displacement** 3,660 tons **Dimensions** 125m x 15m x 7m **Speed** 29 knots **Armament** 1 - 4.5" gun, 4 - 20mm guns, Sea Dart Missile System: 2 - Phalanx, Lynx Helicopter, 6 Torpedo Tubes **Complement** 280 +.

## Notes
Sister Ships SHEFFIELD and COVENTRY lost in 1982 during the Falklands conflict. The first of class for disposal was BIRMINGHAM which paid off in late 1999. She was sold for scrap in October 2000 and towed to Santander in Spain.

**HMS York**

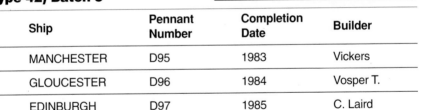

## SHEFFIELD CLASS
### (Type 42) Batch 3

| Ship | Pennant Number | Completion Date | Builder |
|------|----------------|-----------------|---------|
| MANCHESTER | D95 | 1983 | Vickers |
| GLOUCESTER | D96 | 1984 | Vosper T. |
| EDINBURGH | D97 | 1985 | C. Laird |
| YORK | D98 | 1984 | Swan Hunter |

**Displacement** 4,775 tons **Dimensions** 132m x 15m x 7m **Speed** 30 knots + **Armament** 1- 4.5" gun, 2 - Phalanx, 4 - 20mm guns, Sea Dart missile system, Lynx Helicopter, 6 Torpedo Tubes **Complement** 301.

### Notes
"Stretched' versions of earlier ships of this class. Designed to provide area defence of a task force. Deck edge stiffening fitted to counter increased hull stress. YORK to conduct on board trial of Sea Ram inner layer missile defence system throughout 2001. The Type 45 is now being designed to eventually replace this class.

18

WALTER SARTORI

**HMS Sheffield**

# BROADSWORD CLASS
## (Type 22) Batch 2

| Ship | Pennant Number | Completion Date | Builder |
|------|----------------|-----------------|---------|
| BRAVE | F94 | 1985 | Yarrow |
| SHEFFIELD | F96 | 1987 | Swan Hunter |
| COVENTRY | F98 | 1988 | Swan Hunter |

**Displacement** 4,100 tons **Dimensions** 143m x 15m x 6m **Speed** 30 knots **Armament** 2 Sea Wolf Missile Systems, 4 - 30mm + 2 - 20mm guns, 6 Torpedo Tubes, 1 or 2 Lynx Helicopters **Complement** 273.

## Notes
A Sea King can be, and is, carried in some ships of this class. All Batch 1 ships were sold to Brazil 1995-1997. The 1998 Strategic Defence Review resulted in BOXER, BEAVER and LONDON being offered for sale in 1999. BRAVE was laid up in late 1999 at Portsmouth in "Extended Readiness" but is likely to be offered for sale. COVENTRY will be replaced by ST ALBANS at the end of 2001. SHEFFIELD will remain in service until replaced by the Future Surface Combattant, albeit without a surface to surface missile system, which was removed in 2000.

● CROWN COPYRIGHT

**HMS Cumberland**

## BROADSWORD CLASS
### (Type 22) Batch 3

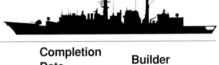

| Ship | Pennant Number | Completion Date | Builder |
|---|---|---|---|
| CUMBERLAND | F85 | 1988 | Yarrow |
| CAMPBELTOWN | F86 | 1988 | C. Laird |
| CHATHAM | F87 | 1989 | Swan Hunter |
| CORNWALL | F99 | 1987 | Yarrow |

**Displacement** 4,200 tons **Dimensions** 147m x 15m x 7m **Speed** 30 knots **Armament** 1 - 4.5" gun, 1 - Goalkeeper, 8 - Harpoon, 2 - Seawolf, 2 - 30mm guns, 6 Torpedo Tubes, 2 Lynx or 1 Sea King Helicopter **Complement** 250.

### Notes
General purpose gun and Goalkeeper system added to these ships as a direct result of lessons learned during Falklands conflict. All these ships have a major anti-submarine capability. Cost £180 million each. All are capable of acting as fleet flagships.

# DUKE CLASS (Type 23)

| Ship | Pennant Number | Completion Date | Builder |
|------|---------------|-----------------|---------|
| KENT | F78 | 2000 | Yarrow |
| PORTLAND | F79 | 2000 | Yarrow |
| GRAFTON | F80 | 1996 | Yarrow |
| SUTHERLAND | F81 | 1997 | Yarrow |
| SOMERSET | F82 | 1996 | Yarrow |
| ST ALBANS | F83 | 2001 | Yarrow |
| LANCASTER | F229 | 1991 | Yarrow |
| NORFOLK | F230 | 1989 | Yarrow |
| ARGYLL | F231 | 1991 | Yarrow |
| MARLBOROUGH | F233 | 1991 | Swan Hunter |
| IRON DUKE | F234 | 1992 | Yarrow |
| MONMOUTH | F235 | 1993 | Yarrow |
| MONTROSE | F236 | 1993 | Yarrow |
| WESTMINSTER | F237 | 1993 | Swan Hunter |
| NORTHUMBERLAND | F238 | 1994 | Swan Hunter |
| RICHMOND | F239 | 1994 | Swan Hunter |

**Displacement** 3,500 tons **Dimensions** 133m x 15m x 5m **Speed** 28 knots **Armament** Harpoon & Seawolf missile systems: 1 - 4.5" gun, 2 - single 30mm guns, 4 - 2 twin, magazine launched, Torpedo Tubes, Helicopter **Complement** 157.

**Notes**
 These are now the backbone of the RN's frigate force after a number of teething difficulties bringing them into operational service. They incorporate 'Stealth' technology to minimise magnetic, radar, acoustic and infra-red signatures. Gas turbine and diesel electric propulsion. NORFOLK was fitted with the new Mk8 Mod 1 4.5 inch gun in Nov 2000.

F231

● MIKE WELSFORD

**HMS Argyll**

● CHRIS ROGERS **HMS Ledbury**

# MINE COUNTERMEASURES SHIPS (MCMV'S) HUNT CLASS

| Ship | Pennant Number | Completion Date | Builder |
|------|---------------|-----------------|---------|
| BRECON | M29 | 1980 | Vosper T. |
| LEDBURY | M30 | 1981 | Vosper T. |
| CATTISTOCK | M31 | 1982 | Vosper T. |
| COTTESMORE | M32 | 1983 | Yarrow |
| BROCKLESBY | M33 | 1983 | Vosper T. |
| MIDDLETON | M34 | 1984 | Yarrow |
| DULVERTON | M35 | 1983 | Vosper T. |
| CHIDDINGFOLD | M37 | 1984 | Vosper T. |
| ATHERSTONE | M38 | 1987 | Vosper T. |
| HURWORTH | M39 | 1985 | Vosper T. |
| BERKELEY | M40 | 1988 | Vosper T. |
| QUORN | M41 | 1989 | Vosper T. |

**Displacement** 625 tonnes **Dimensions** 60m x 10m x 2.2m **Speed** 17 knots **Armament** 1 x 30mm + 2 x 20mm guns **Complement** 45.

## Notes

The largest warships ever built of glass reinforced plastic. Their cost (£35m each) has dictated the size of the class. Very sophisticated ships – and lively seaboats! All based at Portsmouth and Faslane. Ships are frequently deployed in the Fishery Protection role COTTESMORE, BRECON and DULVERTON in the Northern Ireland squadron. BICESTER was sold to Greece and renamed HS EUROPE during mid 2000. BERKELEY is due to follow in February 2001.

**HMS Penzance**

# SANDOWN CLASS

| Ship | Pennant Number | Completion Date | Builder |
|------|----------------|-----------------|---------|
| SANDOWN | M101 | 1989 | Vosper T. |
| INVERNESS | M102 | 1991 | Vosper T. |
| CROMER | M103 | 1991 | Vosper T. |
| WALNEY | M104 | 1992 | Vosper T. |
| BRIDPORT | M105 | 1993 | Vosper T. |
| PENZANCE | M106 | 1998 | Vosper T. |
| PEMBROKE | M107 | 1998 | Vosper T. |
| GRIMSBY | M108 | 1999 | Vosper T. |
| BANGOR | M109 | 2000 | Vosper T. |
| RAMSEY | M110 | 2000 | Vosper T. |

**Displacement** 450 tons **Dimensions** 53m x 10m x 2m **Speed** 13 knots **Armament** 1 - 30mm gun **Complement** 34.

**Notes**

A class dedicated to a single mine hunting role. Propulsion is by vectored thrust and bow thrusters. Up to 15 more ships were planned, but the 7 due to be ordered in 1991 were postponed until 1994. The last two, BLYTH and SHOREHAM will be delivered in 2001.

**HMS Dumbarton Castle**

# PATROL VESSELS
# CASTLE CLASS

| Ship | Pennant Number | Completion Date | Builder |
| --- | --- | --- | --- |
| LEEDS CASTLE | P258 | 1981 | Hall Russell |
| DUMBARTON CASTLE | P265 | 1982 | Hall Russell |

**Displacement** 1,450 tons **Dimensions** 81m x 11m x 3m **Speed** 20 knots **Armament** 1 - 30mm gun **Complement** 40

### Notes

These ships have a dual role – that of fishery protection and offshore patrols within the limits of UK territorial waters. Unlike the Island Class these ships are able to operate helicopters – including Sea King aircraft. LEEDS CASTLE is scheduled to be on long term deployment to the Falkland Islands during 2001 with her ships' company rotating every four months.

**HMS Shetland**

# ISLAND CLASS

| Ship | Pennant Number | Completion Date | Builder |
|------|----------------|-----------------|---------|
| ANGLESEY | P277 | 1979 | Hall Russell |
| ALDERNEY | P278 | 1979 | Hall Russell |
| GUERNSEY | P297 | 1977 | Hall Russell |
| SHETLAND | P298 | 1977 | Hall Russell |
| LINDISFARNE | P300 | 1978 | Hall Russell |

**Displacement** 1,250 tons **Dimensions** 60m x 11m x 4m **Speed** 17 knots
**Armament** 1 - 30mm gun **Complement** 39.

### Notes
Built on trawler lines these ships were introduced to protect the extensive British interests in North Sea oil/gas installations and to patrol the 200 mile fishery limit. All vessels have extra crew members to allow leave to be taken and thus extend vessels time on task over the year. ORKNEY was paid off in April 1999 and sold to the Trinidad and Tobago Defence Force in late 2000.

● CROWN COPYRIGHT

HMS Puncher

# COASTAL TRAINING CRAFT
# P2000 (ARCHER) CLASS

| Ship | Pennant Number | Completion Date | Builder |
|------|----------------|-----------------|---------|
| ARCHER | P264 | 1985 | Watercraft |
| BITER | P270 | 1985 | Watercraft |
| SMITER | P272 | 1986 | Watercraft |
| PURSUER | P273 | 1988 | Vosper |
| TRACKER | P274 | 1998 | Ailsa Troon |
| RAIDER | P275 | 1998 | Ailsa Troon |
| BLAZER | P279 | 1988 | Vosper |
| DASHER | P280 | 1988 | Vosper |
| PUNCHER | P291 | 1988 | Vosper |
| CHARGER | P292 | 1988 | Vosper |
| RANGER | P293 | 1988 | Vosper |
| TRUMPETER | P294 | 1988 | Vosper |

**Displacement** 43 tonnes **Dimensions** 20m x 6m x 1m **Speed** 20 knots **Armament** Nil **Complement** 14.

## Notes
In service with RN University units. TRUMPETER and RANGER deployed to Gibraltar in 1991.

27

**HMS Scott**

# SURVEY SHIPS

| Ship | Pennant Number | Completion Date | Builder |
|------|----------------|-----------------|---------|
| SCOTT | H 131 | 1997 | Appledore |

**Displacement** 13,300 tonnes **Dimensions** 130m x 21.5m x 14m **Speed** 17 knots
**Complement** 63

## Notes

SCOTT carries a mixture of the latest UK and US survey equipment. The sonar system is US supplied. She operates a three watch system whereby the vessel is run by 42 of the ships company of 63 with the remainder on leave. Each crew member works 75 days in the ship before having 30 days off, allowing her to spend more than 300 days at sea in a year. These manpower reductions over previous survey ships have been possible because of the extensive use of commercial lean manning methods including unmanned machinery spaces, fixed fire fighting systems and extensive machinery and safety surveillance technology. In May 2000 she embarked on a 23 month deployment, including a period operating in her secondary role as an MCM forward support unit.

MARITIME PHOTOGRAPHIC

**HMS Roebuck**

| Ship | Pennant Number | Completion Date | Builder |
|------|----------------|-----------------|---------|
| ROEBUCK | H130 | 1986 | Brooke Marine |

**Displacement** 1500 tonnes **Dimensions** 64m x 13m x 4m **Speed** 15 knots **Complement** 47.

### Notes

Survey ship able to operate for long periods away from shore support, this ship and the other vessels of the Hydrographic Fleet collect the data that is required to produce the Admiralty Charts and publications which are sold to mariners worldwide. Fitted with the latest fixing aids and sector scanning sonar.

**HMS Herald**

| Ship | Pennant Number | Completion Date | Builder |
|------|----------------|-----------------|---------|
| HERALD | H138 | 1974 | Robb Caledon |

**Displacement** 2,733 tons **Dimensions** 79m x 15m x 5m **Speed** 14 knots **Complement** 115.

**Notes**
Due to pay off early 2001. HERALD, BEAGLE, BULLDOG and ROEBUCK are to be replaced by two new build survey vessels ordered in 2000. (See page 36)

● D HANNAFORD                                     **HMS Beagle**

# BULLDOG CLASS

| Ship | Pennant Number | Completion Date | Builder |
|---|---|---|---|
| BULLDOG | H317 | 1968 | Brooke Marine |
| BEAGLE | H319 | 1968 | Brooke Marine |

**Displacement** 1,088 tons **Dimensions** 60m x 11m x 4m **Speed** 15 knots
**Complement** 39.

### Notes
Designed to operate in coastal waters. Both have been extensively refitted to extend hull life. BULLDOG is scheduled to pay off in mid- 2001.

HMS Gleaner

## INSHORE SURVEY VESSEL

| Ship | Pennant Number | Completion Date | Builder |
|------|----------------|-----------------|---------|
| GLEANER | H86 | 1983 | Emsworth |

**Displacement** 22 tons **Dimensions** 14.8m x 4.7m x 1.3m **Speed** 14 knots
**Complement** 5.

### Notes
Small inshore survey craft used for the collection of data from the shallowest inshore waters.

● CHRIS ROGERS

**HMS Endurance**

# ICE PATROL SHIP

| Ship | Pennant Number | Completion Date | Builder |
|------|----------------|-----------------|---------|
| ENDURANCE | A171 | 1990 | Ulstein-Hatlo |

**Displacement** 5,129 tons **Dimensions** 91m x 17.9m x 6.5m **Speed** 14.9 knots **Armament** Small arms **Aircraft** 2 Lynx **Complement** 113.

## Notes
Chartered for only 7 months in late 1991 to replace the older vessel of the same name. Originally M/V POLAR CIRCLE, renamed HMS POLAR CIRCLE (A176) and then purchased by MoD(N) and renamed again in October 1992 to current name. Spends 4-6 months each year in South Atlantic supporting British Antarctic Survey.

● MIKE WELSFORD

**Exploit**

## COASTAL TRAINING CRAFT
## ARCHER CLASS

| Ship | Pennant Number | Completion Date | Builder |
|------|----------------|-----------------|---------|
| EXPRESS | A163 | 1988 | Vosper T |
| EXPLORER | A164 | 1985 | Watercraft |
| EXAMPLE | A165 | 1985 | Watercraft |
| EXPLOIT | A167 | 1988 | Vosper T |

**Displacement** 43 tons **Dimensions** 20m x 6m x 1m **Speed** 20 knots **Armament** Nil
**Complement** 14

**Notes**
Former Example Class Training vessels for the RNXS - until the organisation was disbanded on 31 March 1994. Vessels were then transferred to RN University Units as sea training tenders. (See also page 27)

34

● DAVE CULLEN

**RV Triton**

# RESEARCH VESSEL

| Ship | Pennant Number | Completion Date | Builder |
|------|----------------|-----------------|---------|
| TRITON | - | 2000 | Vosper Thornycroft |

**Displacement** 1100 tons **Dimensions** 98m x 22.5m x 3.2m **Speed** 20 knots
**Complement** 12 crew + 12 scientific personnel

## Notes

Launched 6 May 2000 and handed over in August 2000. Operated by DERA the vessel is a two third scale demonstrator described as the most significant advance in naval design since the Dreadnoughts. The vessel is being used to explore the potential of the advanced trimaran hull form. If successful, the design could form the basis of the Future Surface Combattant.

# SHIPS ORDERED FOR THE FUTURE FLEET...

**ASTUTE/AMBUSH/ARTFUL -** The in service date (ISD) for ASTUTE is now June 2005, a slippage of 42 months. An order for a further two vessels is anticipated in due course. The average production cost for each of the five submarines is £508m.

**ALBION/BULWARK** -The ISDs for ALBION and BULWARK are now March and December 2003 respectively. The total cost of the Landing Platform (Dock) LPD programme is now put at £631m, an increase of £16m since the order was placed. ALBION will cost £359m and BULWARK £272m.

**TYPE 45** - It was announced in July 2000, that "subject to the satisfactory outcome of negotiations", the government "intends to place an order" for three Type 45 destroyers. To be known as the Daring class the first two would be named DARING and DAUNT-LESS. Hulls 1 and 3 would be built by prime contractor BAE Systems, whilst hull 2 would be built by Vosper Thornycroft. It is expected they will be the first of a class of "up to" 12 ships. An order for a second batch is likely to be placed around 2004.

**TYPE 23** - The final unit of the class ST. ALBANS is fitting out at BAE Systems Govan yard and is expected to complete in late 2001.

**SURVEY VESSELS** - A £130m order was placed with prime contractor Vosper Thornycroft in June 2000 to build two new survey ships. The 3,500 tonne vessels will be built by sub-contractor Appledore Shipbuilding Ltd. To be named ECHO and ENTERPRISE they are due to enter service in 2002 and 2003 respectively.

**SINGLE ROLE MINEHUNTER** - The final two SRMH are completing at Vosper Thornycroft. BLYTH was launched on 4 July 2000 and is due to be delivered in 2001. SHOREHAM is due to be launched in April 2001 and delivered in December 2001.

**ALTERNATE LANDING SHIPS LOGISTIC** - An order for 4 ALSLs was announced in October 2000. Based on the Dutch ROTTERDAM LPD design, two are to be built by Swan Hunter on the Tyne and two by BAE Systems at Govan.

**RO-RO CONTAINER SHIPS** - Also announced in October 2000 was the long awaited contract for the supply of 6 Ro-Ro ferries to meet the requirement for strategic sealift capability. Under a 25 year Private Finance Initiative contract AWSR Shipping Ltd will build and run the vessels for the MoD. Four of the ships are to be built by Flensberger in Germany, with the remaining two to be built by Harland and Wolff, Belfast.

**RFA WAVE CLASS TANKERS** - WAVE KNIGHT was launched at BAE Systems Barrow-in-Furness yard in September 2000 and is expected to be accepted in October 2001, entering service in February 2002. WAVE RULER is scheduled to be launched in February 2001 and enter service in November 2002.

# THE ROYAL FLEET AUXILIARY

The Royal Fleet Auxiliary Service (RFA) is a civilian manned fleet owned and operated by the Ministry of Defence. Its main task is to supply warships of the Royal Navy at sea with fuel, food, stores and ammunition which they need to remain operational while away from base. The service also provides aviation support and training facilities for the Royal Navy – together with amphibious support and secure sea transport for for the Royal Marines and British Army units.

The RFA is the largest single employer of UK merchant navy officers and ratings. Although the ethos is very much based on that of the Merchant Service, the personnel undergo a considerable overlay of naval training, in the main to provide them with a greater degree of survivability when operating their ships in hostile waters. Such training includes the operation and maintenance of close range and small calibre weapons and decoys (self-defence weapons), firefighting and damage control. But, fundamental to the success of the RFA is the need for competent seamen to undertake replenishment at sea and small boat operations, and to man ships flight decks to ensure the safe operation of helicopters.

The service prides itself that each ship is available for operations for approximately 80% of the year. Unlike the Royal Navy, officers and men of the RFA join a vessel for a period of time - say six months - and do not expect to be in port for leave periods at all during this period.

Throughout 2000 and despite ongoing industrial action by some of its members, the Service maintained its standing commitment to provide tankers, giving vital fuel support, in the West Indies, Falklands and the Gulf. The two strategic lift ships SEA CENTURION and SEA CRUSADER continued to ferry heavy military equipment and armoured vehicles to Thessaloniki, for use by British troops in Kosovo. The LSLs have been particularly busy operating with the Amphibious Ready Group (ARG). After exercises in the Gulf and Mediterranean SIR BEDIVERE and SIR TRISTRAM were diverted, with the ARG to support operations in Sierra Leone. SIR PERCIVALE spent the last 6 months of 2000 berthed in Freetown, supporting UK forces on the ground and is likely to remain until April at least. The ARG was again diverted to Sierra Leone in November, this time it included ARGUS, FORT AUSTIN, BRAMBLELEAF and SIR GERAINT. FORT GEORGE deployed to the Gulf with the ILLUSTRIOUS Task Group in January and was diverted to provide humanitarian aid to Mozambique in the wake of flooding and to operations off Sierra Leone in support of the carrier. Naval Task Group 2000, a round the world deployment, left the UK in May supported by FORT VICTORIA, BAYLEAF and DILIGENCE. Early on in the deployment BAYLEAF was diverted to Sierra Leone and DILIGENCE escorted the defective TIRELESS to Gibraltar. BAYLEAF was again diverted to Sierra Leone on the return leg of NTG 2000 to support the second ARG deployment! FORT GRANGE left Croatia in January after nearly 3 years alongside in Split supporting British forces there. Her return to the UK was short lived; following a refit, and a renaming to FORT ROSALIE she sailed to Gibraltar to provide accommodation for the crew of TIRELESS and repair teams where she remained at the end of the year. The demands upon RFA resources were demonstrated by the fact that OLNA was briefly brought out of reserve in Gibraltar to help fill the gaps left by the operations off West Africa. OLNA and OLWEN were however laid up for sale at the end of 2000.

There is still no news on the purchase of dedicated Primary Casualty Receiving ships, although ARGUS, FORT GEORGE and FORT VICTORIA are all to have their medical facilities considerably enhanced. What implications this will have for possible new ships remains to be seen.

## SHIPS OF THE ROYAL FLEET AUXILIARY
### Pennant Numbers

| Ship | Pennant Number | Ship | Pennant Number | Ship | Pennant Number |
|---|---|---|---|---|---|
| BRAMBLELEAF | A81 | ARGUS | A135 | FORT GEORGE | A388 |
| SEA CRUSADER | A96 | GREY ROVER | A269 | SIR BEDIVERE | L3004 |
| SEA CENTURION | A98 | GOLD ROVER | A271 | SIR GALAHAD | L3005 |
| BAYLEAF | A109 | BLACK ROVER | A273 | SIR GERAINT | L3027 |
| ORANGELEAF | A110 | FORT ROSALIE | A385 | SIR PERCIVALE | L3036 |
| OAKLEAF | A111 | FORT AUSTIN | A386 | SIR TRISTRAM | L3505 |
| DILIGENCE | A132 | FORT VICTORIA | A387 | | |

# KEEP UP TO DATE THROUGHOUT THE YEAR

Warship World is published six times a year (Jan, Mar, May, Jul, Sep, Nov) and gives you all the information necessary to keep this book updated throughout the year.

**RFA Oakleaf**

## SUPPORT TANKERS

| Ship | Pennant Number | Completion Date | Builder |
|------|----------------|-----------------|---------|
| OAKLEAF | A111 | 1981 | Uddevalla |

**Displacement** 49,310 tons **Dimensions** 173.7m x 32.2m x 11.2m **Speed** 14 knots **Complement** 35.

### Notes
At 49,310 tons displacement, she is the largest vessel in RN/RFA service.

● DAVE CULLEN

**RFA Orangeleaf**

# LEAF CLASS

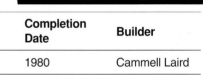

| Ship | Pennant Number | Completion Date | Builder |
|------|----------------|-----------------|---------|
| BRAMBLELEAF | A81 | 1980 | Cammell Laird |
| BAYLEAF | A109 | 1982 | Cammell Laird |
| ORANGELEAF | A110 | 1982 | Cammell Laird |

**Displacement** 37,747 tons **Dimensions** 170m x 26m x 12m **Speed** 14.5 knots **Complement** 60.

## Notes

All are ex merchant ships, originally acquired for employment mainly on freighting duties. All have been modified to enable them to refuel warships at sea. One of the class is normally permanently on station in the Gulf in support of Armilla Patrol and allied warships. BRAMBLELEAF is MoD(N) owned, the remainder on long-term bareboat charter. All are commercial Stat32 class tankers.

● CROWN COPYRIGHT

**RFA Black Rover**

# ROVER CLASS

| Ship | Pennant Number | Completion Date | Builder |
|------|----------------|-----------------|---------|
| GREY ROVER | A269 | 1970 | Swan Hunter |
| GOLD ROVER | A271 | 1974 | Swan Hunter |
| BLACK ROVER | A273 | 1974 | Swan Hunter |

**Displacement** 11,522 tons **Dimensions** 141m x 19m x 7m **Speed** 18 knots **Armament** 2 - 20mm guns **Complement** 49/54

**Notes**

Small Fleet Tankers designed to supply warships with fresh water, dry cargo and refrigerated provisions, as well as a range of fuels and lubricants. Helicopter deck, but no hangar. Have been employed in recent years mainly as support for HM Ships operating around the Falkland Islands and West Indies, spending up to two years on deployment in these areas. There are currently no plans to replace these three ships before 2007.

**RFA Fort Rosalie**

# STORES VESSELS
# FORT CLASS I

| Ship | Pennant Number | Completion Date | Builder |
|------|----------------|-----------------|---------|
| FORT ROSALIE | A385 | 1978 | Scott Lithgow |
| FORT AUSTIN | A386 | 1979 | Scott Lithgow |

**Displacement** 23,384 tons **Dimensions** 183m x 24m x 9m **Speed** 20 knots
**Complement** 201, (120 RFA, 36 MoD Civilians & 45 RN).

**Notes**
Full hangar and maintenance facilities are provided and up to four Sea King helicopters can be carried for both the transfer of stores and anti-submarine protection of a group of ships. Both ships can be armed with 4 - 20mm guns mounted on the Scot platforms.

**RFA Fort George**

# REPLENISHMENT SHIPS
# FORT CLASS II

| Ship | Pennant Number | Completion Date | Builder |
|------|----------------|-----------------|---------|
| FORT VICTORIA | A387 | 1992 | Harland & Wolff |
| FORT GEORGE | A388 | 1993 | Swan Hunter |

**Displacement** 31,500 tons **Dimensions** 204m x 30m x 9m **Speed** 20 knots **Armament** 4 - 30mm guns, 2 x Phalanx CIWS, Sea Wolf Missile System (Fitted for but not with) **Complement** 100 (RFA), 24 MoD Civilians, 32 RN and up to 122 aircrew.

**Notes**
 "One stop" replenishment ships with the widest range of armaments, fuel and spares carried. Can operate up to 5 Sea King Helicopters with full maintenance facilities onboard. Flight deck facilities frequently used as training area for helicopter crews. Medical facilities to be upgraded for Primary Casualty Reception Ship duties (on a limited scale).

● STEVE BUSH

**RFA Sir Tristram**

# LANDING SHIPS (LOGISTIC)
# SIR CLASS

| Ship | Pennant Number | Completion Date | Builder |
|------|---------------|-----------------|---------|
| SIR BEDIVERE | L3004 | 1967 | Hawthorn |
| SIR GALAHAD | L3005 | 1987 | Swan Hunter |
| SIR GERAINT | L3027 | 1967 | Stephen |
| SIR PERCIVALE | L3036 | 1968 | Hawthorn |
| SIR TRISTRAM | L3505 | 1967 | Hawthorn |

**Displacement** 5,550 tons **Dimensions** 126m x 18m x 4m **Speed** 17 knots **Armament** Can be fitted with 20 or 40mm guns in emergency **Complement** 65, (SIR GALAHAD is larger at 8,451 tons. 140m x 20m **Complement** 58 ).

## Notes
Manned by the RFA but tasked by the Army, these ships are used for heavy secure transport of stores – embarked by bow and stern doors. Can operate helicopters from both vehicle and flight deck if required and carry 340 troops. SIR TRISTRAM was rebuilt after extensive Falklands War damage. After extensive delays, SIR BEDIVERE completed a Ship Life Extension Programme (SLEP) at Rosyth in 1998. She is now 7,700 tonnes displacement and her dimensions are 137 x 20 x 4 metres. Occasionally used for MCMV support.

44

**RFA Sea Crusader**

# RO-RO VESSELS

| Ship | Pennant Number | Completion Date | Builder |
|---|---|---|---|
| SEA CRUSADER | A96 | 1996 | Kawasaki Heavy Industries |

**Displacement** 25,500 tonnes **Dimensions** 164m x 25m x 6.5m **Speed** 18 knots **Complement** 17

**Notes**
A commercial Roll on-Roll off cargo ship, chartered while under construction in Japan. Arrived in UK in November 1996, her main role being a heavy-lift ship for the Joint Rapid Reaction Force. Routinely employed on freighting runs transporting armoured vehicles and equipment to the Mediterranean, and continental ports. 2,500 lane metres of vehicle capacity available. Originally due to be returned to her owners in October 1998 her MoD charter has however been extended as an interim measure until new Ro-Ro ships become available in 2004. (See page 36).

45

**RFA Sea Centurion**

| Ship | Pennant Number | Completion Date | Builder |
|------|----------------|-----------------|---------|
| SEA CENTURION | A 98 | 1998 | Societa Esercizio Cantieri |

**Displacement** 21,000 tonnes **Dimensions** 183m x 26m x 7m **Speed** 22 knots **Complement** 18

### Notes

First of class of a new generation of Ro-Ro ships, Stena 4-runner class on bareboat charter from Stena from new-build, initially for 18 months with options to extend. Joined the RFA in October 98 for service with the JRDF. Routinely used for freighting military vehicles and equipment. 2715 lane metres on three cargo decks, accessed by a large stern ramp and internal ramps.

**RFA Diligence**

# FORWARD REPAIR SHIP

| Ship | Pennant Number | Completion Date | Builder |
|------|----------------|-----------------|---------|
| DILIGENCE | A132 | 1981 | Oesundsvarvet |

**Displacement** 5,814 tons **Dimensions** 120m x 12m x 3m **Speed** 15 knots **Armament** 2 - 20mm **Complement** RFA 40, RN Personnel – approx 100.

**Notes**
Formerly the M/V STENA INSPECTOR purchased (£25m) for service in the South Atlantic. Her deep diving complex was removed and workshops added. When not employed on "repair ship" duties can serve as support vessel for MCMVs and submarines on deployment.

47

**RFA Argus**

## AVIATION TRAINING SHIP

| Ship | Pennant Number | Completion Date | Builder |
|---|---|---|---|
| ARGUS | A135 | 1981 | Cantieri Navali Breda |

**Displacement** 28,081 tons (full load) **Dimensions** 175m x 30m x 8m **Speed** 18 knots **Armament** 4 - 30 mm, 2 - 20 mm **Complement** 254 (inc 137 Air Group) **Aircraft** 6 Sea King, 12 Harriers can be carried in a "ferry role".

### Notes
Formerly the M/V CONTENDER BEZANT taken up from trade during the Falklands crisis. Purchased in 1984 (£13 million) for conversion to an 'Aviation Training Ship'. A £50 million re-build was undertaken at Belfast from 1984-87. Undertook rapid conversion in October 1990 to "Primary Casualty Reception Ship" (Hospital Ship!) for service in the Gulf. These facilities are being enhanced and made permanent during early 2001.

48

HMS ILLUSTRIOUS at Malta

Crown Copyright

RFA SIR GALAHAD

Dave Cullen

HMS COTTESMORE converted for Northern Ireland duties

HMS KENT

RFA ARGUS and Sea King HAS 6

**HMS RANGER - a Gibraltar based P2000**

Crown Copyright

HMS MANCHESTER firing a Sea Dart Missile

Crown Copyright

Crown Copyright

Trident Sunset

# MARINE SERVICES SUPPORT

The Chief Executive Naval Bases and Supply Agency (NBSA) is tasked by the Defence Logistic Organisation (DLO) with Tri-Service provision of Marine Services and is responsible for In and Out-of-Port maritime services in support of Naval Bases, CinC Fleet, The Meteorological Office, DERA, RAF and Army. Their role is to undertake Mooring and Navigation buoy maintenance, freighting of Naval armaments and explosives, maritime support to the DERA underwater research programme and sea-borne services to the Fleet. Maritime services at the Kyle of Lochalsh are provided primarily to support the BUTEC Ranges, and secondarily to fulfil Fleet requirements in that area.

In the three main ports at Portsmouth, Devonport and Clyde the service is currently delivered under a Government Owned/Commercially Operated (GOCO) contract with Serco Denholm Ltd. The vessels being operated on a BARECON (Bareboat charter) basis.

For Naval Armament Freighting, Mooring Maintenance, RMAS NEWTON and services at Kyle of Lochalsh, the service is currently delivered by the General Manager RMAS from his HQ at Pembroke Dock.

For both RAF training and Range Safety Clearance duties at Army and MoD ranges throughout Britain, services are currently delivered under two separate Government Owned/Commercially Operated (GOCO) contracts.

Marine Services vessels can be seen at work in the UK Naval Bases and are easily identified by their black hulls, buff coloured superstructure and by their Flag, which in the case of GM RMAS vessels, is a blue ensign defaced in the fly by a yellow anchor over two wavy lines. The remaining vessels fly the 'Other Government' ensign. Which is a blue ensign defaced in the fly by a yellow anchor.

# SHIPS OF
# THE MARINE SERVICES
## Pennant Numbers

| Ship | Pennant Number | Page | Ship | Pennant Number | Page |
|------|----------------|------|------|----------------|------|
| CAMERON | A72 | 78 | BUSTLER | A225 | 60 |
| MELTON | A83 | 73 | CAPABLE | A226 | 60 |
| MENAI | A84 | 73 | CAREFUL | A227 | 60 |
| MEON | A87 | 73 | FAITHFUL | A228 | 60 |
| DALMATIAN | A129 | 61 | DEXTEROUS | A231 | 60 |
| TORNADO | A140 | 76 | ADAMANT | A232 | 72 |
| TORMENTOR | A142 | 76 | SHEEPDOG | A250 | 61 |
| WATERMAN | A146 | 75 | LADYBIRD | A253 | 67 |
| FRANCES | A147 | 63 | NEWHAVEN | A280 | 69 |
| FLORENCE | A149 | 63 | NUTBOURNE | A281 | 69 |
| GENEVIEVE | A150 | 63 | NETLEY | A282 | 69 |
| KITTY | A170 | 62 | OBAN | A283 | 70 |
| LESLEY | A172 | 62 | ORONSAY | A284 | 70 |
| HUSKY | A178 | 61 | OMAGH | A285 | 70 |
| MASTIFF | A180 | 61 | PADSTOW | A286 | 71 |
| SALUKI | A182 | 61 | ILCHESTER | A308 | 73 |
| SALMOOR | A185 | 77 | INSTOW | A309 | 73 |
| SALMAID | A187 | 77 | IXWORTH | A318 | 73 |
| SETTER | A189 | 61 | COLLIE | A328 | 61 |
| JOAN | A190 | 62 | IMPULSE | A344 | 59 |
| BOVISAND | A191 | 68 | IMPETUS | A345 | 59 |
| CAWSAND | A192 | 68 | NEWTON | A367 | 64 |
| HELEN | A198 | 63 | WARDEN | A368 | 79 |
| MYRTLE | A199 | 62 | KINTERBURY | A378 | 66 |
| SPANIEL | A201 | 61 | FALCONET | Y01 | 80 |
| NORAH | A205 | 61 | PETARD | Y02 | 80 |
| FORCEFUL | A221 | 60 | OILPRESS | Y21 | 74 |
| NIMBLE | A222 | 60 | MOORHEN | Y32 | 78 |
| POWERFUL | A223 | 60 | MOORFOWL | Y33 | 78 |
| ADEPT | A224 | 60 | | | |

**MV Impulse**

# TUGS
# IMPULSE CLASS

| Ship | Pennant Number | Completion Date | Builder |
|------|----------------|-----------------|---------|
| IMPULSE | A344 | 1993 | Dunston |
| IMPETUS | A345 | 1993 | Dunston |

**G.R.T.** 400 tons approx **Dimensions** 33m x 10m x 4m **Speed** 12 knots
**Complement** 5.

## Notes
Completed in 1993 specifically to serve as berthing tugs for the Trident Class sub-marines at Faslane. Both operated under contract by Serco Denholm.

**MV Faithful**

# TWIN UNIT TRACTOR TUGS (TUTT'S)

| Ship | Pennant Number | Completion Date | Builder |
|------|----------------|-----------------|---------|
| FORCEFUL | A221 | 1985 | R. Dunston |
| NIMBLE | A222 | 1985 | R. Dunston |
| POWERFUL | A223 | 1985 | R. Dunston |
| ADEPT | A224 | 1980 | R. Dunston |
| BUSTLER | A225 | 1981 | R. Dunston |
| CAPABLE | A226 | 1981 | R. Dunston |
| CAREFUL | A227 | 1982 | R. Dunston |
| FAITHFUL | A228 | 1985 | R. Dunston |
| DEXTEROUS | A231 | 1986 | R. Dunston |

**G.R.T.** 375 tons **Dimensions** 39m x 10m x 4m **Speed** 12 knots **Complement** 9.

**Notes**

The principal harbour tugs in naval service. All operated under contract by Serco Denholm except CAPABLE at Gibraltar which is managed locally.

60

**MV Dalmatian**

# DOG CLASS

| Ship | Pennant Number | Ship | Pennant Number |
|------|----------------|------|----------------|
| DALMATIAN | A129 | SETTER | A189 |
| HUSKY | A178 | SPANIEL | A201 |
| MASTIFF | A180 | SHEEPDOG | A250 |
| SALUKI | A182 | COLLIE | A328 |

**G.R.T.** 152 tons **Dimensions** 29m x 8m x 4m **Speed** 12 knots **Complement** 5.

**Notes**

General harbour tugs – all completed between 1965 and 1969. COLLIE is classified as a trials vessel - operated by Serco Denholm and based at Kyle of Lochalsh but for disposal 2001.

● MARITIME PHOTOGRAPHIC

**MV Kitty**

## TRITON CLASS

| Ship | Pennant Number | Ship | Pennant Number |
|------|----------------|------|----------------|
| KITTY | A170 | JOAN | A190 |
| LESLEY | A172 | MYRTLE | A199 |
| LILAH  • | A174 | NORAH | A205 |

**G.R.T.** 89 tons **Speed** 8 knots **Complement** 4.

**Notes**
Known as Water Tractors these craft are used for basin moves and towage of light barges. Operated by Serco Denholm Ltd. • Awaiting disposal.

**MV Florence**

# FELICITY CLASS

| Ship | Pennant Number | | Ship | Pennant Number |
|------|----------------|---|------|----------------|
| FRANCES | A147 | | FLORENCE | A149 |
| FIONA | A148 | | GENEVIEVE | A150 |
| HELEN | A198 | | | |

**G.R.T.** 80 tons **Speed** 10 knots **Complement** 4.

## Notes
Water Tractors used for the movement of small barges and equipment. All are operated by Serco Denholm. Two sister vessels (GEORGINA and GWENDOLINE) sold to Serco Denholm in 1996 for service in H M Naval bases. FIONA on disposal list 2001.

**RMAS Newton**

# RESEARCH VESSELS

| Ship | Pennant Number | Completion Date | Builder |
|------|----------------|-----------------|---------|
| NEWTON | A367 | 1976 | Scotts |

**G.R.T.** 2,779 tons **Dimensions** 99m x 16m x 6m **Speed** 15 knots **Complement** 27

**Notes**
Primarily used in the support of RN training exercises. Some limited support provided for various trials. Operated by the RMAS.

**MV Colonel Templer**

| Ship | Pennant Number | Completion Date | Builder |
|---|---|---|---|
| COLONEL TEMPLER | | 1966 | Hall Russell |

**Displacement** 1,300 tons  **Dimensions** 56m x 11m x 5.6 m  **Speed** 12 knots
**Complement** 14

### Notes

Built as a stern trawler but converted in 1980 for use by the Defence Evaluation and Research Agency as an acoustic research vessel. A major rebuild was completed after a serious fire gutted the ship in 1990. 12 scientists can be carried. From Nov 2000 owned by MoD and to be operated on the Clyde by Serco Denholm in 2001. To assume some of SALMASTER's extra duties.

**RMAS Kinterbury**

## NAVAL ARMAMENT VESSELS

| Ship | Pennant Number | Completion Date | Builder |
|------|----------------|-----------------|---------|
| KINTERBURY | A378 | 1981 | Appledore SB |

**G.R.T.** 1,357 tons **Dimensions** 64m x 12m x 5m **Speed** 14 knots **Complement** 11.

### Notes
Two holds carry Naval armament stores, ammunition and guided missiles. In addition to freighting tasks it is also used for trials work and in support of RN exercises. ARROCHAR laid up at Portsmouth and expected to be sold during 2001.

**MV Ladybird**

| Ship | Pennant Number | Completion Date | Builder |
|---|---|---|---|
| LADYBIRD | A253 | 1973 | Beverley |

**G.R.T.** 279 tons **Dimensions** 34m x 8m x 3m **Speed** 10.5 knots **Complement** 7-9.

**Notes**
A Naval Armament carrier operated by Serco Denholm. BEE is on the Disposal List at Portsmouth. COCKCHAFER sold 2000.

**MV Bovisand**

# TENDERS
# STORM CLASS

| Ship | Pennant Number | Completion Date | Builder |
|------|----------------|-----------------|---------|
| BOVISAND | A191 | 1997 | FBM (Cowes) |
| CAWSAND | A192 | 1997 | FBM (Cowes) |

**G.R.T** 225 tonnes **Dimensions** 23m x 11m x 2m **Speed** 15 knots **Complement** 5

**Notes**
These craft are used in support of Flag Officer Sea Training (FOST) at Plymouth to transfer staff quickly and comfortably to and from Warships and Auxiliaries within and beyond the Plymouth breakwater in open sea conditions. These are the first vessels of a small waterplane area twin hull (SWATH) design to be ordered by the Ministry of Defence and cost £6.5 million.

**MV Nutbourne**

## NEWHAVEN CLASS

| Ship | Pennant Number | Completion Date | Builder |
|---|---|---|---|
| NEWHAVEN | A280 | 2000 | Aluminium Shipbuilders Ltd |
| NUTBOURNE | A281 | 2000 | Aluminium Shipbuilders Ltd |
| NETLEY | A282 | 2001 | Aluminium Shipbuilders Ltd |

**Tonnage** 77 tonnes (45 grt) **Dimensions** 18.3m x 6.8m x 1.88m **Speed** 10 knots **Complement** 3 Crew (60 passengers).

### Notes
Twin hulled MCA Class IV Passenger Vessels based at Portsmouth. Replacements for Fleet tenders. Employed on general passenger duties.

**MV Oban**

## OBAN CLASS

| Ship | Pennant Number | Completion Date | Builder |
|------|----------------|-----------------|---------|
| OBAN | A283 | 2000 | McTay |
| ORONSAY | A284 | 2000 | McTay |
| OMAGH | A285 | 2000 | McTay |

**Tonnage** 199 tons **Dimensions** 27.7m x 7.30m x 3.75m **Speed** 10 knots **Complement** 7 Crew (60 passengers).

**Notes**
New MCA Class IIA Passenger Vessels to replace Fleet tenders. Employed on general passenger duties on the Clyde.

**MV Padstow**

| Ship | Pennant Number | Completion Date | Builder |
| --- | --- | --- | --- |
| PADSTOW | A286 | 2000 | Aluminium Shipbuilders Ltd |

**Tonnage** 77 tonnes (45 grt) **Dimensions** 18.3m x 6.8m x 1.88m **Speed** 10 knots **Complement** 3 Crew (60 passengers).

### Notes
Twin hulled MCA Class VIA Passenger Vessel based at Plymouth. Used on general passenger ferrying duties and in support of FOST seariders.

**MV Adamant**

| Ship | Pennant Number | Completion Date | Builder |
|------|---------------|-----------------|---------|
| ADAMANT | A232 | 1992 | FBM (Cowes) |

**G.R.T** 170 tonnes **Dimensions** 30m x 8m x 1m **Speed** 22 knots  **Complement** 5

**Notes**
Twin catamaran hulls based on the commercial Red Jet design (as used by Red Funnel Ferry Co). First water jet propulsion vessel owned by MoD(N). In service as a Clyde personnel ferry - operated by Serco Denholm.

**MV Meon**

| Ship | Pennant Number | Ship | Pennant Number |
|------|----------------|------|----------------|
| MELTON | A83 | INSTOW • | A309 |
| MENAI | A84 | IRONBRIDGE • | A311 |
| MEON | A87 | IXWORTH • | A318 |
| ILCHESTER • | A308 | HEADCORN | A1766 |

**G.R.T.** 78 tons **Dimensions** 24m x 6m x 3m **Speed** 10.5 knots **Complement** 4/5.

**Notes**

Vessels marked • are diving tenders. Remainder are Training Tenders, Passenger Ferries, or Cargo Vessels. All except MELTON are operated by Serco Denholm. IRONBRIDGE and IXWORTH are RN manned. MILFORD, LAMLASH, LECHLADE, HEVER, HARLECH, HAMBLEDON, HOLMWOOD and HORNING for disposal in 2001.

● DANE MURDOCH

**MV Oilpress**

# COASTAL OILER

| Ship | Pennant Number | Completion Date | Builder |
|------|----------------|-----------------|---------|
| OILPRESS | Y21 | 1969 | Appledore Shipbuilders |

**G.R.T.** 362 tons **Dimensions** 41m x 9m x 3m **Speed** 11 knots **Complement** 5.

**Notes**
Employed as Harbour and Coastal Oiler. Operated by Serco Denholm on the Clyde.

**MV Waterman**

# WATER CARRIER

| Ship | Pennant Number | Completion Date | Builder |
|------|----------------|-----------------|---------|
| WATERMAN | A146 | 1978 | R. Dunston |

**G.R.T.** 263 tons **Dimensions** 40m x 8m x 2m **Speed** 11 knots **Complement** 5.

**Notes**
Capable of coastal passages, but normally supplies either demineralised or fresh water to the Fleet within port limits. WATERFOWL is owned and operated by Serco Denholm.

● MIKE WELSFORD

**MV Tormentor**

# TORPEDO RECOVERY VESSELS (TRV)
# TORNADO CLASS

| Ship | Pennant Number | Completion Date | Builder |
|---|---|---|---|
| TORNADO | A140 | 1979 | Hall Russell |
| TORMENTOR | A142 | 1980 | Hall Russell |

**G.R.T.** 560 tons **Dimensions** 47m x 8m x 3m **Speed** 14 knots **Complement** 13.

### Notes
All vessels have had suitable rails fitted to enable them to operate as exercise minelayers in addition to their torpedo recovery role. TORRENT was sold in 2000 to Nigeria for commercial service.

**RMAS Salmoor**

# MOORING & SALVAGE VESSELS
## SAL CLASS

| Ship | Pennant Number | Completion Date | Builder |
|------|----------------|-----------------|---------|
| SALMOOR | A185 | 1985 | Hall Russell |
| SALMAID | A187 | 1986 | Hall Russell |

**Displacement** 2200 tonnes **Dimensions** 77m x 15m x 4m **Speed** 15 knots **Complement** 19

### Notes
Multi-purpose vessels designed to lay and maintain underwater targets, navigation marks and moorings. SALMASTER placed on Disposal List in Nov 2000 and laid up at Greenock for sale.

**MV Moorfowl**

## MOOR CLASS

| Ship | Pennant Number | Completion Date | Builder |
|------|----------------|-----------------|---------|
| MOORHEN | Y32 | 1989 | McTay Marine |
| MOORFOWL | Y33 | 1989 | McTay Marine |
| CAMERON | A72 | 1991 | Richard Dunston |

**Displacement** 518 tons **Dimensions** 32m x 11m x 2m **Speed** 8 knots **Complement** 10

### Notes
Powered mooring lighters for use within sheltered coastal waters. CAMERON is similar but was sold to DERA at Dunfermline in 1996 and is employed as an Underwater Trials & Experimental vessel at Rosyth. Operated by Briggs Marine on behalf of DERA. MOORHEN based at Portsmouth and MOORFOWL at Devonport. Both vessels also undertake coastal work.

**MV Warden**

# TRIALS VESSEL

| Ship | Pennant Number | Completion Date | Builder |
|------|----------------|-----------------|---------|
| WARDEN | A368 | 1989 | Richards |

**Displacement** 626 tons **Dimensions** 48m x 10m x 4m **Speed** 15 knots **Complement** 11.

### Notes
Built as a Range Maintenance Vessel but now based at Kyle of Lochalsh and operated by the RMAS in support of BUTEC. Note removal of gantry and extended bridge structure.

● STEVE BUSH         **Spitfire**

## LONG RANGE RECOVERY AND SUPPORT CRAFT (LRRSC)

| Ship | Pennant Number | Completion Date | Builder |
|------|--------|------------|---------|
| SEAL | 5000 | 1967 | Brooke Marine |
| SEAGULL | 5001 | 1970 | Fairmile Const. |

**G.R.T.** 251 tons **Dimensions** 36.6m x 7.16m x 1.8m **Speed** 21 knots **Complement** 8. Both are based at Invergordon.

## RESCUE AND TARGET TOWING LAUNCHES (RTTL)

SPITFIRE, HALIFAX, HAMPDEN, HURRICANE, LANCASTER & WELLINGTON

**G.R.T.** 60 tons **Dimensions** 24m x 5.6m x 1.6m **Speed** 21 knots **Complement** 4/6
They are based at Great Yarmouth and Plymouth.

### Notes
The primary tasks for RAF Support craft include target towing, winch training helicopter crews for SAR and the vessels are also used for sea survival training of aircrew. Vessels on this page are operated under contract by GFE AV Seawork.

● STEVE BUSH                                    **RCTV Andalsnes**

# RAMPED CRAFT LOGISTIC

| Vessel | Pennant Number | Completion Date | Builder |
|--------|----------------|-----------------|---------|
| ARROMANCHES | L105 | 1987 | James & Stone |
| ANDALSNES | L107 | 1984 | James & Stone |
| AKYAB | L109 | 1984 | James & Stone |
| AACHEN | L110 | 1986 | James & Stone |
| AREZZO | L111 | 1986 | James & Stone |
| AUDEMER | L113 | 1987 | James & Stone |

**Displacement** 165 tons **Dimensions** 33m x 8m x 1.5m **Speed** 9 knots
**Complement** 6.

### Notes

Smaller – "all purpose" landing craft capable of carrying up to 96 tons. In service in coastal waters around Cyprus and UK. ARROMANCHES was formerly AGHEILA (re-named 1994 when original vessel was sold). Several vessels sport green and black camouflage scheme. The larger ARDENNES and ARAKAN sold for commercial service in Nigeria 2000.

# AIRCRAFT OF THE FLEET AIR ARM

## European Helicopter Industries EH101 MERLIN

**Variants:** HM1
**Role:** Anti-submarine and Maritime patrol
**Engine:** 3 x Rolls-Royce Turbomeca RTM322 turboshafts developing 2,100 shp
**Length:** 74' 10" Width: 14' 10" Height: 21' 10" Main rotor: 61'
**Max Speed:** 167 kts   Range: 625 nm
**Crew:** 3 (Pilot, Observer and Aircrewman)
**Avionics:** Blue Kestrel 360 degree search radar, Orange Reaper ESM, passive and active sonar systems and AQS903 digital processor.
**Armament:** 4 lightweight torpedoes or depth charges.
**Squadron service:** 700M (Merlin IFTU), 824 squadron
**Notes:** The Merlin HM1 is the replacement for the anti-submarine Sea King HAS Mk 6. It is the first Royal Naval derivative of the EH101 helicopter, designed and produced under a collaborative programme by UK's GKN Westland Helicopters Ltd and Italy's helicopter manufacturer, Agusta. Merlin was designed to operate from both large and small ship's flight decks, in severe weather and high sea states, by day and night.
It is expected that the first front line squadron and Type 23 frigate Flights should be ready to deploy during 2001.

# British Aerospace SEA HARRIER

**Variants:** FA2
**Role:** Short take off, vertical landing (STOVL) fighter attack and reconnaissance aircraft.
**Engine:** 1 x 21,500lb thrust Rolls Royce PEGASUS 104, turbofan.
**Span** 25' 3" **Length** 49' 1" **Height** 12' 0" **Max weight** 26,200lb.
**Max speed** Mach .9 540 knots **Crew** 1 pilot.
**Avionics:** Blue Vixen pulse doppler radar
**Armament:** Up to 4 x AMRAAM Air to Air Missiles. SIDEWINDER air to air missiles. 2 - 30mm Aden cannons with 120 rounds per gun in detachable pods, one either side of the lower fuselage. 1 fuselage centreline and 4 underwing hardpoints. The inner wing stations are capable of carrying 2,000lb of stores and are plumbed for drop tanks. The other positions can carry stores up to 1,000lb in weight. Possible loads include 1,000lb or practice bombs; 190 or 100 gallon drop tanks. A single F95 camera is mounted obliquely in the nose for reconnaissance.
**Squadron Service:** 800, 801 and 899 squadrons in commission.
**Notes:** A radical shift in the operational command of Sea Harriers took place with the formation of Joint Force 2000. On 1 April 2000 the Royal Navy's FA2s were joined with the RAF's GR7s, under the command of a Rear Admiral, together with other maritime air assets. The Sea Harriers will continue to be based at Yeovilton until 2003, when they will move to RAF Cottesmore/RAF Wittering to co-locate with Harrier GR7s. During 2001, 800 Naval Air Squadron (NAS) will embark in HMS INVINCIBLE and 801 NAS in HMS ILLUSTRIOUS. 899 NAS is responsible for the training of pilots and maintainers and the development of tactics. It is normally shore based at Yeovilton. In a period of tension it could embark to reinforce the embarked air groups in the carriers.

# Westland SEA KING

Developed for the Royal Navy from the Sikorsky SH3D, the basic Sea King airframe is used in three different roles. The following details are common to all:

**Engines:** 2 x 1600shp Rolls Royce Gnome H 1400 – 1 free power turbines.

**Rotor Diameter** 62' 0" **Length** 54' 9" **Height** 17' 2" **Max Weight** 21,400lb **Max Speed** 125 knots.

The 3 versions are:-

CROWN COPYRIGHT

# HAR 5 : HAS 6

The HAS6 has improved sonics, deeper dipping active sonar and ESM

**Roles:** Anti-submarine search and attack. SAR. Transport.

**Crew:** 2 pilots, 1 observer and 1 aircrewman.

**Avionics:** Sea Searcher radar; Type 2069 variable depth active/passive sonar AQS 902 passive sonobuoy analyser. Orange Crop passive ESM equipment.

**Armament:** 4 fuselage hardpoints capable of carrying STINGRAY torpedoes or depth charges. Various flares, markers, grenades and sonobuoys can be carried internally and hand launched. A 7.62mm machine gun can be mounted in the doorway.

**Squadron Service:** 771 Squadron operates the HAR 5. 810, 819, and 820 squadrons are in commission equipped with HAS 6.

**Notes:** The Sea King has been the backbone of the Fleet Air Arm's anti-submarine force since 1970. 810 squadron at Culdrose provides advanced and operational flying training, with the capability to embark to reinforce the front line. 819 is shore based at Prestwick The HAR 5 has an excellent SAR capability which is frequently demonstrated in the south west approaches. The HAS 6 has less complete SAR facilities when full ASW equipment fitted.

● CROWN COPYRIGHT

# AEW 2

**Role:** Airborne Early Warning. **Crew:** 1 pilot and 2 observers.
**Avionics:** Thorn/EMI Searchwater radar  Orange Crop passive ESM equipment.
**Squadron Service:** 849 HQ, 849A and 849B Flights in commission.
**Notes:** Used to detect low flying aircraft trying to attack aircraft carrier battle groups under conventional shipborne radar cover. Can also be used for surface search utilising its sophisticated, computerised long range radar. During 2001 849A Flight will be embarked in HMS INVINCIBLE and 849B Flight in HMS ILLUSTRIOUS. 849HQ acts as a training and trials unit at Culdrose.

# HC 4

**Role:** Commando assault and utility transport.
**Crew:** 2 pilots and 1 aircrewman.
**Armament:** Door mounted 7.62mm machine gun.
**Squadron Service:** 845, 846 and 848 squadrons in commission.
**Notes:** The HC4 has a fixed undercarriage with no sponsons or radome.Can carry up to 27 troops in the cabin or underslung loads up to 6,000lb in weight. All squadrons are based at Yeovilton but embark or detach at short notice to support 3 Cdo Brigade. 845 Sqn has had aircraft based in Split in support of UN and NATO Forces in Bosnia since1993.

● CROWN COPYRIGHT

# Westland LYNX

**Variants:** HAS 3, HAS 3S, HMA 8.
**Roles:** Surface search and attack; anti-submarine attack; SAR; troop carrying.
**Engines:** 2 x 900hp Rolls Royce GEM BS 360-07-26 free shaft turbines.
**Rotor diameter:** 42' 0" **Length** 39' 1" **Height** 11' 0" **Max Weight** 9,500lb.
**Max Speed:** 150 knots. **Crew:** 1 pilot and 1 observer.
**Avionics:** SEA SPRAY radar. Orange Crop passive ESM equipment. Sea Owl Passive Infrared Device (Mk 8).
**Armament:** External pylons carry up to 4 - SEA SKUA air to surface missiles or 2 x STINGRAY torpedoes, depth charges and markers.
**Squadron Service:** 702 and 815 squadrons in commission.

**Notes:** 815 OEU is a trials Flight for HMA 8 aircraft. 702 is the training squadron . 815 squadron is the parent unit for single aircraft ships flights. Both squadrons are based at Yeovilton. All ships' flight aircraft are being converted to HMA 8 specification. Full delivery of 59 conversions is expected by 2003.
Another version of the Lynx, the AH7, is operated by Royal Marines in 847 NAS.

# Westland GAZELLE AH1

**Engine:** 1 x 592shp Turbomeca ASTAZOU free power turbine.
**Crew:** 1 or 2 pilots.

**Notes:** The Gazelle AH1 is used by 847 NAS based at Yeovilton as a spotter/communications aircraft for the Royal Marines.

# OTHER AIRCRAFT TYPES IN ROYAL NAVY SERVICE DURING 2001

## British Aerospace HAWK

**Engine:** 1 x Ardour Mk 151 5200 lbs thrust.
**Crew:** 1 or 2 Pilots (both service and civilian)
**Notes:** With FRADU at Culdrose to provide support for training of RN ships, RN flying standards flight and as airborne targets for the aircraft direction school.

● CROWN COPYRIGHT

## British Aerospace JETSTREAM T2 and T3

**Engines:** 2 x 940hp Turbomeca ASTAZOU 16D turboprops. (T3 Garrett turboprops).
**Crew:** 1 or 2 pilots, 2 student observers plus 3 other seats.
**Notes:** T2's are used by 750 squadron at Culdrose for training Fleet Air Arm Observers.T3's are used by the Heron flight at Yeovilton for operational support/communications flying.

● CROWN COPYRIGHT (STUART ANTROBUS)

## Aerospatiale  AS365N DAUPHIN 2

**Engines:** 2 x Turbomeca Arriel 1C1.
**Crew:** 1 or 2 pilots.
**Notes:** Operated by British International from Plymouth City Airport under MoD contract. Used to transfer Sea Training staff from shore and between ships operating in the Plymouth sea training areas during work-ups.

● SHORTS

# GROB G115 D-2

Used for the flying grading and conversion of Rotary to Fixed Wing pilots. They are owned and operated by a division of Short Brothers plc and operate from Plymouth City Airport.

## Royal Navy Historic Flight

The RNHF is supported financially by the Swordfish Heritage Trust. The Historic Flight has been civilianised since 1993.

The current holding of aircraft is:

**Flying:** 2 Fairey Swordfish, 1 Fairey Firefly,1 Sea Hawk (under repair), 1 Sea Fury.
**Static Display:** 1 Fairey Swordfish

# WEAPONS OF THE ROYAL NAVY
## Sea Launched Missiles

◀

### Trident II D5

The American built Lockheed Martin Trident 2 (D5) submarine launched strategic missiles are Britain's only nuclear weapons and form the UK contribution to the NATO strategic deterrent. 16 missiles, each capable of carrying up to 6 UK manufactured thermonuclear warheads (but currently limited to 4 under current government policy), are aboard each of the Vanguard class SSBNs. Trident has a maximum range of 12,000 km and is powered by a three stage rocket motor. Launch weight is 60 tonnes, overall length and width are 13.4 metres and 2.1 metres respectively.

### Sea Wolf

Short range rapid reaction anti-missile and anti-aircraft weapon. The complete weapon system, including radars and fire control computers, is entirely automatic in operation. Type 22 frigates carry two sextuple Sea Wolf launchers but the subsequent Type 23 frigates carry 32 Vertical Launch Seawolf (VLS) in a silo on the foredeck. Basic missile data: weight 82 kg, length 1.9 m, wingspan 56 cm, range c.56 km, warhead 13.4 kg. The VLS missile is basically similar but has jettisonable tandem boost rocket motors.

## Harpoon

The Boeing (McDonnell Douglas) Harpoon is a sophisticated anti-ship missile using a combination of inertial guidance and active radar homing to attack targets out to a range of 130 km, cruising at Mach 0.9 and carrying a 227 kg warhead. Currently fitted to the Batch II Type 22 and Type 23 frigates. It is powered by a lightweight turbojet but is accelerated at launch by a booster rocket. The Royal Navy also deploys the UGM-84 submarine launched version aboard its Swiftsure and Trafalgar class SSNs.

# Sea Dart

A medium range area defence anti aircraft missile powered by a ramjet and solid fuel booster rocket. Maximum effective range is in the order of 80 km and the missile accelerates to a speed of Mach 3.5. It forms the main armament of the Type 42 destroyers and was originally fitted to the Invincible class carriers. Missile weight 550 kg, length 4.4 m, wingspan 0.91 m.

# Tomahawk (BGM-109)

This is a land attack cruise missile with a range of 1600 km and can be launched from a variety of platforms including surface ships and submarines. Some 65 of the latter version were purchased from America to arm Trafalgar class SSNs with the first being delivered to the Royal Navy for trials during 1998. Tomahawk is fired in a disposal container from the submarine's conventional torpedo tubes and is then accelerated to its subsonic cruising speed by a booster rocket motor before a lightweight F-107 turbojet takes over for the cruise. Its extremely accurate guidance system means that small targets can be hit with precision at maximum range, as was dramatically illustrated in the Gulf War. Total weight of the submarine version, including its launch capsule is 1816 kg, it carries a 450 kg warhead, length is 6.4 metres and wingspan (fully extended) 2.54 m. Fitted in some S & T class submarines.

# Air Launched Missiles

## Sea Skua

A small anti ship missile developed by British Aerospace arming the Lynx helicopters carried by various frigates and destroyers. The missile weighs 147 kg, has a length of 2.85 m and a span of 62 cm. Powered by solid fuel booster and sustainer rocket motors, it has a range of over 15 km at high subsonic speed. Sea Skua is particularly effective against patrol vessels and fast attack craft, as was demonstrated in both the Falklands and Gulf Wars.

## Sidewinder

This is one of the world's most successful short range air to air missiles. The latest AIM-9L version carried by Sea Harriers uses a heat seeking infra red guidance system and has a range of 18 km. Powered by a solid fuel rocket motor boosting it to speeds of Mach 2.5, it weighs 86.6 kg and is 2.87 m long.

## AMRAAM

The Hughes AIM-120 Advanced Medium Range Air To Air Missile arms the latest Sea Harrier FA.2 and has a range of around 50 km. Weight 157 kg, length 3.65 m. Coupled with the Blue Vixen multi mode radar, the AMRAAM gives a substantial boost to the aircraft's capability as an air defence interceptor, allowing Beyond Visual Range (BVR) engagements.

# Guns

## 114mm Vickers Mk8

The Royal Navy's standard medium calibre general purpose gun which arms the later Type 22s, Type 23 frigates and Type 42 destroyers. Rate of fire: 25 rounds/min. Range: 22,000 m. Weight of Shell: 21 kg.

## Goalkeeper

A highly effective automatic Close in Weapons System (CIWS) designed to shoot down missiles and aircraft which have evaded the outer layers of a ships defences. The complete system, designed and built in Holland, is on an autonomous mounting and includes radars, fire control computers and a 7-barrel 30 mm Gatling gun firing 4200 rounds/min. Goalkeeper is designed to engage targets between 350 and 1500 metres away.

## Phalanx

A US built CIWS designed around the Vulcan 20 mm rotary cannon. Rate of fire is 3000 rounds/min and effective range is c.1500 m. Fitted in Type 42, HM Ships OCEAN and FEARLESS.

## GCM-AO3 30mm

This mounting carries two Oerlikon 30 mm guns each capable of firing 650 rounds/min. Effective range is 3000 m. Fitted to Type 22 frigates and the LPDs.

## DS30B 30mm

Single 30 mm mounting carrying an Oerlikon 30 mm gun. Fitted to Type 23 frigates and various patrol vessels and MCMVs.

## GAM BO 20mm

A simple hand operated mounting carrying a single Oerlikon KAA 200 automatic cannon firing 1000 rounds/min. maximum range is 2000 m. Carried by most of the fleet's major warships except the Type 23 frigates.

## 20mm Mk.7A

The design of this simple but reliable weapon dates back to World War II but it still provides a useful increase in firepower, particularly for auxiliary vessels and RFAs. Rate of fire 500-800 rounds/min.

# Torpedoes

## Stingray

A lightweight anti submarine torpedo which can be launched from ships, helicopters or aircraft. In effect it is an undersea guided missile with a range of 11 km at 45 knots or 7.5 km at 60 knots. Length 2.1 m, diameter 330 mm. Aboard Type 42s and Type 22s Stingray is fired from triple tubes forming part of the Ships Torpedo Weapon System (STWS) but the newer Type 23s have the Magazine Torpedo Launch System (MTLS) with internal launch tubes.

## Mk24 Tigerfish

A wire guided heavyweight torpedo carried by all Royal Navy submarines. Mainly designed for the anti-submarine role but its 134 kg warhead is equally effective against surface vessels. Propulsion is by means of a powerful two speed electric motor giving a range of 29 km at 24 knots or 13 km at 35 knots. Diameter is the standard 533 mm, and overall length approximately 6.5 m.

## Spearfish

A complex heavyweight torpedo now entering service after a protracted and extensive development period. Claimed by the manufacturers to be the world's fastest torpedo, capable of over 70 kts, its sophisticated guidance system includes an onboard acoustic processing suite and tactical computer backed up by a command and control wire link to the parent submarine. Spearfish is fired from the standard submarine torpedo tube, but it is slightly shorter than Tigerfish and utilises an advanced turbine engine for higher performance.

# At the end of the line ...

Readers may well find other warships afloat which are not mentioned in this book. The majority have fulfiled a long and useful life and are now relegated to non-seagoing duties. The following list gives details of their current duties:

| Pennant No | Ship | Remarks |
| --- | --- | --- |
| | BRITANNIA | Ex Royal Yacht at Leith. Open to the public. |
| A134 | RAME HEAD | Escort Maintenance Vessel – Royal Marines Training Ship in Fareham Creek (Portsmouth) |
| C35 | BELFAST | World War II Cruiser Museum ship – Pool of London Open to the public daily Tel: 0171-407 6434 |
| D23 | BRISTOL | Type 82  Destroyer – Sea Cadet Training Ship at Portsmouth. |
| D73 | CAVALIER | World War II Destroyer & Oberon class Submarine Museum Ships at Chatham. Partially open to the public Tel: 01634 823800 |
| S17 | OCELOT | |
| F126 | PLYMOUTH | Type 12 Frigate & Oberon class Submarine Museum Ships at Birkenhead, Wirral. Open to the public daily. Tel: 0151 650 1573 |
| S21 | ONYX | |
| M1115 | BRONINGTON | Ton Class Minesweeper at Manchester Limited Opening to the Public Tel 0161 877 7778 |
| S67 | ALLIANCE | Submarine – Museum Ship at Gosport Open to the public daily. Tel: 01705 511485 |
| M1151 | IVESTON | (Thurrock)　　　　} Static Sea Cadet |
| M1154 | KELLINGTON | (Stockton upon Tees)　} Training Vessels |

**At the time of publishing (December 2000) the following ships were laid up in long term storage or awaiting sale.**

| PORTSMOUTH | PLYMOUTH | ROSYTH |
| --- | --- | --- |
| Arrochar | Courageous | Churchill |
| Beaver | Conqueror | Dreadnought |
| Boxer | Valiant | Revenge |
| London | Warspite | Swiftsure |
| Orwell | | Resolution |
| Olna | | Renown |
| Olwen | | Repulse |
| Scylla | | |

96